APPRENTICESHIP PROGRAM FOR MOS OF ELECTRICIAN

WORK EXPERIENCE LOG

APPRENTICE NAME _____

DEPARTMENT OF THE NAVY
HEADQUARTERS UNITED STATES MARINE CORPS
WASHINGTON , D.C. 20380

TABLE OF CONTENTS

INTRODUCTION

APPRENTICESHIP

Apprenticeship is training for jobs in technical trades that require special skills and knowledge. It involves technical schooling and planned on-the-job training under supervision. For young workers desiring to gain a skilled occupation, the apprenticeship program provides a step by step program of instruction and on-the-job training. This program will lead to advance standing in the technical skill or trade you have chosen.

The USMC Apprenticeship Program provides you with the opportunity to meet some requirements for advancement in your chosen skill area while on active duty. As you progress in your training in the Marine Corps and master the skills required of your trade, you will have the mastered skills recorded in your log. Your apprenticeship program allows you to make your work experience on the Marine Corps count twice. First, to fulfill your active duty obligation in a productive manner. Second, to provide you with a usable skill if you should decide to return to civilian life. By having documented proof of Marine Corps schooling and work experience, you should qualify for a better job at higher pay.

Most apprenticeship terms range from 1 to 4 years, depending upon the trade involved. To master a particular trade requires: (1) Learning all or most of the skills of the trade; (2) Perfecting each specific skill; (3) Bringing each skill up to the speed and accuracy required of the job; and (4) Learning to use specific skills in combination with other skills.

MARINE CORPS APPRENTICESHIP PROGRAM

The purpose of establishing the Marine Corps Apprenticeship Program is to provide Marine Corps commanders an opportunity to implement programs of apprenticeship for military personnel in occupations closely related and applicable to private industry needs and requirements. Marine Corps school training and experience in the field will, if properly documented, satisfy private industry requirements for the training of apprentices in nationally recognized apprenticeable occupations.

The ultimate objective of the United States Marine Corps Apprenticeship Program is to provide registered certification of an individual Marine's skilled craft occupational training. The program has been designed to achieve recognition for Marines equal to their civilian counterparts.

1

Registration of the National Apprenticeship Standards for the United States Marine Corps with the Bureau of Apprenticeship and Training, U.S. Department of Labor, is beneficial to the Marine Corps, to individual Marines, and to private industry, management and labor. Acceptance of U.S. Marine Corps apprentices as skilled craft-workers by private industry, management, and labor will enhance Marines' employment opportunities as veterans, shorten the term of private industry apprenticeship through the award of appropriate credit for previous military training experience, and provide a source of registered skilled personnel to meet national manpower requirements.

THE ELECTRICIAN APPRENTICESHIP PROGRAM

The purpose of this pamphlet is to announce the United States Marine Corps Apprenticeship Program for the trade of Electrician.

Policies and procedures for participation in the program are contained in MCO 1550.22.

Marines holding a primary or secondary 1141 MOS and who are serving in that MOS may participate in the program.

This is an 8000 hour program which leads to a certification of journeyman in the trade of Electrician by the U.S. Department of Labor. Participation in the program is voluntary, and no membership in labor unions or professional associations is required. The work process schedule and schedule of related instruction are outlined in pages 8 through 11. The purpose of the work process schedule and the schedule of related instruction is as indicated below:

> The work process schedule reflects categories of work experience required by Marine apprentices to qualify as Journeyman Electrician.

> The schedule of related instruction identifies courses which are available to Marine apprentices to satisfy the 144 hours of annual related instruction required for completion of the program.

Marines eligible for the program may enroll by contacting the Unit or Base Education Officer who will assist in the preparation of the application.

Apprentice logs and instructions on their use will be
provided by the Education Officer at the time of registration. Marine apprentices will be required to maintain
their log sheets on a daily basis. Log entries must be
verified by the Marine apprentice's immediate supervisor
on a weekly basis.

Marines who have partially completed an approved Federal
or State registered civilian apprenticeship will be awarded
credit within the constraints of the individual apprenticeship training program standards. Each training hour suc-
cessfully completed in the occupation involved will be
awarded credit upon presentation of authenticated documentation. Marines serving beyond their initial enlistment
are considered career Marines, and may make application
for the apprenticeship program in order to be certified as
having completed an apprentice program. Career Marine
apprentices must complete the same requirements as the first-
term apprentice except that they will be given credit for
one-half the hours required for the specific apprenticeship
program in which they are enrolled provided their previous
enlistment was served in an MOS applicable to the relevant
apprenticeship program for which applying.

Organized related instruction for all United States Marine
Corps apprentices will be defined by the individual apprenticeship program standards. Such related instruction will
be provided on an hour-per-year basis, or the total hours
may be achieved through the successful completion of a
multi-week training course for the apprenticeable occupation
involved at any United States Marine Corps training school,
or other Service School (Army, Navy, etc.) providing such
training.

Upon successful completion of apprenticeship training
and experience requirements as prescribed by individual
apprenticeship program standards, the apprentice will submit
a request via the chain of command, accompanied by a letter
from the appropriate commander or education officer, to
the Office of National Industry Promotion, Bureau of Apprenticeship and Training, U.S. Department of Labor, Washington,
D.C. 20213, for issuance of a Certificate of Completion
of Apprenticeship (Enclosure 10). The Bureau of Apprenticeship and Training will issue all Certificates of Completion
of Apprenticeship to the individual through Headquarters,
U.S. Marine Corps (Code OTTE) to the appropriate commander.

3

NATIONAL APPRENTICESHIP STANDARDS

FOR

THE UNITED STATES MARINE CORPS

Developed by Headquarters, United States
Marine Corps, Washington, D. C., with the
assistance of *the Bureau of Apprenticeship
and Training*, Employment and Training
Administration, United States Department
of Labor, Washington, D. C.

AUTHORITY

National Apprenticeship Standards for the United States
Marine Corps are established by authority of:

W. GRAHAM CLAYTOR JR.
Secretary of the Navy

RAY MARSHALL
Secretary, United States
Department of Labor

LOUIS H. WILSON
Commandant of the
Marine Corps

Registered as incorporating the basic standards
recommended by the Bureau of Apprenticeship and
Training, Employment and Training Administration,
United States Department of Labor.

HUGH C. MURPHY
Administrator
Bureau of Apprenticeship and Training
Employment and Training Administration

DEFINITIONS

1. EMPLOYER------------------The United States Marine Corps.

2. PROGRAM SUPERVISOR------Commanding Officer,
   Marine Corps Engineer School,
   Marine Corps Base,
   Camp Lejeune, North Carolina 28542

3. NATIONAL APPRENTICESHIP
   STANDARDS----------------The entire document which embodies
   the procedures for the selection
   and training of Marine Corps apprentices and sets forth all the conditions associated therewith, in-
   cluding training on the job, related technical instruction, and ad-
   ministrative responsibilities.

4. WORK EXPERIENCE LOG-----A book issued to each registered
   apprentice identifying the occu-
   pation, work process training
   schedule, hours allocated to each
   training task increment in the
   work process schedule, and supervisory certification requirements.

5. APPRENTICE---------------Any individual who is on active
   duty in the U.S. Marine Corps,
   meets entry age requirements,
   performs assignments that include
   training in an apprenticeable
   occupation and who is registered
   with the Bureau of Apprenticeship
   and Training, U.S. Department of
   Labor, Washington, D.C..

6. REGISTRATION AGENCY-----The Bureau of Apprenticeship and
   Training, U.S. Department of
   Labor, Washington, D.C..

7. WORK PROCESS SCHEDULE---An outline of work procedures
   which specifies the required
   supervised work experience,
   training on the job, and the
   approximate time to be spent in
   each major process.

8. SCHEDULE OF RELATED INSTRUCTION --- Organized, related and supplemental instruction necessary to provide apprentices with knowledge in technical subjects related to the trade. The instruction may include supervised correspondence or self-study courses, as approved by law or by policy of the registration agency. A minimum of 144 hours each year of apprenticeship training is required. It may also include resident instruction at a DOD or civilian school. Normally, a minimum of 144 hours annually is required. However resident, formal schooling can satisfy total requirements for related instruction if over 360 hours are attained.

WORK PROCESS SCHEDULE FOR THE TRADE OF

ELECTRICIAN

(DOT 824.261-010)

1. **Participant Designation.** Marines working in the military occupational specialty (MOS) 1141 are authorized to participate in the program.

2. **Job Description.** As a result of formal training received in conjunction with MOS qualification, participants are knowledgeable in: use and care of hand tools; use and care of power tools; laying out materials and equipment on job sites; installing service entrances/distribution panels; cutting wire, cable, conduit and raceway; installing and connecting switching outlets and junction boxes; installing conduit systems; testing interior electrical circuits; loading balance interior circuits; calculating proper wire size; installing and connecting various types of fixtures; tracing polarity of conductors and devices; determining appropriate grounding methods; selecting required transformers; connecting transformers in series; installing fuses in systems; repairing all kinds of electrical work; selecting correct motors; connecting pole-phase motors; performing motor operational tests; and performing minor maintenance on motors and control equipment.

WORK EXPERIENCE FUNCTIONS

Hours

A. PRELIMINARY WORK 600

-- Learn names and uses of equipment, to include kind, size,
   and use of cable, wire, boxes, conduits, various switches,
   cut-outs and receptacles.
-- Learn names, uses, and care of hand power tools used in
   assembling electrical materials; maintain special purpose
   equipment and tools used on interior electrical work.

B. RESIDENTIAL AND COMMERCIAL ROUGH WIRING 2500

-- Select proper material from supply.
-- Lay out materials and equipment on job site in accordance
   with blue-prints.
-- Cut wire, cable, conduit, and raceway; thread and ream con-
   duit, bore and cut chases under the direction of supervisor
   (Journeyman).
-- Install service entrance/distribution panel.
-- Install armored and nonmetallic sheathed cable.
-- Install and connect switches, outlets, junction boxes, plugs,
   and light fixtures with proper methods of splicing.
-- Install conduit systems.
-- Install service switches or load centers connecting these
   parts, run raceways, pull in conductors under direction of
   supervisor (Journeyman)
-- Test interior electrical circuit for proper operation
   using proper electrical instruments and test equipment.

C. RESIDENTIAL AND COMMERCIAL FINISH WORK 1500

-- Inventory interior wiring materials to determine if
   materials provided are as required per specifications.
-- Load balance interior circuits.
-- Compute the circuit total connected load per phase.
-- Determine individual load arrangement on circuit to achieve
   a balanced circuit condition.
-- Calculate proper wire size and types of fuses to support
   circuit.
-- Lay out the circuit in accordance with the specifications.
-- Install and connect various types of fixtures.
-- Connect service entrance conductors and devices.
-- Trace polarity of conductors and devices.
-- Determine appropriate grounding method and requirements,
   and test circuit to locate and correct job defects.
-- Inspect interior electrical system/components installation
   for compliance with specifications and the rules of
   National Board of Fire Underwriters and appropriate local
   regulations.

D. INDUSTRIAL LIGHTING AND SERVICE INSTALLATIONS 2,000

-- Install rigid conduit, electric thinwall metallic tubing, BX armored cable, and wiremolds on all types of heavy electrical equipment and major size service entrance installations.
-- Select required transformer.
-- Connect single transformers into system.
-- Connect transformers in series.
-- Parallel single-phase transformers.
-- Parallel three-phase transformers.
-- Connect transformers in banks.
-- Connect transformers for special application.
-- Adjust transformers.
-- Install fuses in system.
-- Install wiring and remote controls for air conditioning.

E. TROUBLESHOOTING 1,000

-- Repair all kinds of electrical work.
-- Check out trouble and make repairs under direction of supervisor/journeyman.
-- Check out trouble and make repairs without supervision.

F. MOTOR INSTALLATION AND CONTROL 400

-- Select correct motor to support given requirements.
-- Connect single-phase motors.
-- Connect poly-phase motors.
-- Install motor controller.
-- Select correct motor protective devices.
-- Align motors in accordance with manufacturers' specification and other requirements.
-- Perform motor operational test.
-- Perform minor maintenance on motors and control equipment.

TOTAL HOURS 8,000

SCHEDULE OF RELATED INSTRUCTION

A total of 144 hours of related instruction is required in order to complete this program. Completion of any one or combination of the below listed courses which equals 144 hours of related instruction or more may be taken to satisfy this requirement. Credit for courses not listed below may be awarded upon presentation of authenticated documentation of satisfactory completion. A synopsis of the course must be submitted with documentation. Documentation and synopsis for courses not listed below will be forwarded to the organizational Education Officer.

Course Number	Course Title	School	Resident	Non-Resident	Hours Credit
NA	Basic Electrical Course	MCES	X		220
NA	Journeyman Electrical Course	MCES	X		320
11.16	Fundamentals of Electricity	MCI		X	17
11.19	Installation Operation and Operators Maintenance of Diesel Engine Driven Generator Set	MCI		X	9
EN 111	Interior Wiring	ACCF, USATSC Newport News VA		X	12
EN 112	Electrical Distribution	SAME AS ABOVE		X	10
EN 113	Construction Print Reading	SAME AS ABOVE		X	10
EN 120	Basic Mathematics	SAME AS ABOVE		X	12
EN 552	Electricity I (Fundamentals) (Incl. Safety)	SAME AS ABOVE		X	14

11

INSTRUCTIONS FOR COMPLETING WORK EXPERIENCE LOG

This pamphlet is issued to each registered apprentice and identifies the occupation, work process training schedules, hours allocated to each training task increment in the work process schedule and supervisory certification requirement.

1. **Marine applicant will:**

   a. Complete the apprentice registration application (enclosure 1) in triplicate. Forward one copy to CMC (Code OTTE), one copy placed in Marine's Service Record Book (SRB), and the third copy is to be retained by the Education Officer.

      (1) Submit the application to the commanding officer or his authorized representative.

      (2) Obtain work experience log, which includes the Work Experience Functions. Obtain one year's supply (12 Copies) of the Apprentice Work Experience Hourly Record, (enclosure 2) from the commanding officer or education officer.

      (3) Complete the Personal History Form, (enclosure 3) and forward to CMC (Code OTTE) with enclosure (1).

      (4) Complete Military Education, (enclosure 4), and forward a certified copy to CMC (Code OTTE) with enclosure (1).

      (5) Complete Civilian Education, (enclosure 5), with certification from the Marine's Service Record Book and forward to CMC (Code OTTE) with enclosure (1).

      (6) Maintain Military Assignment, (enclosure 6).

      (7) Civilian Occupation, (enclosure 7), if applicable, submit statement to program sponsor on employer letterhead, giving length of employment, position held, and manner of performance.

   b. Career oriented apprentice Marines must complete the same requirements as the first-term apprentice except that they will be given credit for only half the hours required for the specific program in which they are enrolled. This is provided their previous enlistment was served in as MOS applicable to the relevant apprenticeship program for which they are applying.

(1) A certified photocopy of enclosure (6) of the work log will be forwarded with the registration application to CMC (Code OTTE).

(2) The Commanding Officer or his designated representative will assign credit hours for previous work experience in accordance with MCO 1550.22 and mark accordingly block 16 of enclosure (1).

2. Procedures for recording hourly work experience

a. Daily Record: Daily entries will be made by the apprentice.

b. Weekly certification by supervisor: Weekly certification will be completed by the shop chief for whom the Marine works.

c. Consolidation/Certification on Month/Yearly recapitulation: The signature line of the work experience hourly record will be signed by the commanding officer or his representative. This report will reflect the entries for the monthly work experience, enclosure (8) of work experience log.

3. Semiannual progress interview

a. Report to your unit Education Officer within 5 to 8 months after date of this application and twice a year thereafter. Enclosure (9) will be completed and forwarded to CMC (Code OTTE).

b. The purpose of the interview is to determine the status of the apprentice and to certify a photocopy of the last hourly record of work experience.

c. The Commanding Officer or Education Officer/authorized representative will sign the Apprentice Progress/Status Report (enclosure (9)).

4. Interruption of Assignment

a. Rifle Range/Leave. Record on the experience hourly record the days away from regular assigned duty.

b. Separation from Active Duty. Status report will be submitted to CMC (Code OTTE) identifying the Marine as being discharged. Upon request, CMC will forward the records to Bureau of Apprenticeship and Training in the Marine's home state of record.

c. Sickness and hospitalization. Recorded by day on the Apprentice Work Experience Hourly Record.

d. Voluntary Disenrollment. An apprentice must request suspension or cancellation. Suspension retains the apprentice in a temporary status for no more than one year. A request for suspension may be mailed directly to CMC (Code OTTE) by the apprentice. Cancellation removes the apprentice from the apprenticeship program. A request for cancellation requires the signature of the apprentice's Commanding Officer or Education Officer.

5. <u>Documentation Required to Validate Related Instruction</u>. Certification of completion or transcript of grades will be used to award credit hours toward completion of the apprenticeship program.

6. <u>Loss of work experience log</u>

a. Request a reissue of a blank log from the Education Officer of your command.

b. Request CMC (Code OTTE) to furnish data available in your records to bring the log up to date.

APPRENTICE REGISTRATION APPLICATION (1500)
NAVMC 11013 (3-77)
SM: 0000-00-006-6800 U/I: SM

1. Print or type.
2. Prepare in triplicate.
3. Forward original and one copy to CMC (Code OTTE).
4. Apprentice retains one copy in Work Experience Log.

PRIVACY ACT NOTIFICATION

Under the authority of Title 5, U.S. Code, Section 301, the information regarding your former and present active military service, educational background and present personal data is requested in order to review and evaluate your qualifications for the Department of Labor apprenticeship program for active-duty Marine Corps personnel. Your Social Security Number is used for purposes of individual identification. This information will be retained by the Commandant of the Marine Corps (Code OTTE) and by the Bureau of Apprenticeship and Training, U.S. Department of Labor, and will not be divulged without your written authorization to anyone other than Headquarters Marine Corps and Department of Labor personnel involved with administration of this program. You are not required to provide this information; however, failure to do so may result in your not being registered for an apprenticeable trade.

APPLICANT INFORMATION

1. NAME (Last, first, middle)

2. SSN

3. DATE OF BIRTH (Day, Month, Year)

4. SEX
   ☐ MALE   ☐ FEMALE

5. RACE/ETHNIC GROUP
   ☐ CAUCASIAN/WHITE   ☐ NEGRO/BLACK   ☐ AMERICAN INDIAN   ☐ SPANISH AMERICAN   ☐ ORIENTAL   ☐ INFORMATION NOT AVAILABLE   ☐ NOT ELSEWHERE CLASSIFIED

6. NAME AND LOCATION OF HIGH SCHOOL FROM WHICH GRADUATED   OR, STATE AND DATE OF GED EQUIVALENCY

7. Did you serve on active duty on or after 5 August 1964 and before 8 May 1975?   ☐ YES   ☐ NO

8. HOME OF RECORD (State)

9. APPRENTICEABLE TRADE FOR REGISTRATION (Give complete title)

10. DOT CODE FOR APPRENTICEABLE TRADE

11. APPRENTICE PROGRAM

I agree to report to the education officer within 5 to 8 months after date of this application and twice a year thereafter. I understand that my registration is voluntary and that registration does not guarantee work or duty assignments appropriate to my apprenticeship. I have read and understand the Privacy Act Statement.

12. Signature of applicant _____   13. Date _____

TO BE FILLED IN BY APPLICANT'S COMMANDING OFFICER OR EDUCATION OFFICER

TO: Commandant of the Marine Corps (Code OTTE), Headquarters U.S. Marine Corps, Washington, D.C. 20380

14. FROM

15. Total hours required for term of apprenticeship   _____ hours

16. Hours credit given for previous work experience   (-) _____ hours

17. Total hours remaining for term of apprenticeship   _____ hours

18. COMMENTS (If any)

19. SIGNATURE OF REGISTRAR
The applicant has been counseled as to the conditions and requirements of the apprenticeship.

Signature _____

20. TITLE

21. DATE

INSTRUCTIONS FOR APPRENTICE REGISTRATION APPLICATION

Item No.

1. Self-explanatory.

2. Enter Social Security Number. Example: 399-03-6433

3. Enter date of birth: Day, Month, Year.

4. Self-explanatory.

5. Self-explanatory

6. Self-explanatory.

7. A check "X" in the YES block signifies that the registrant is regarded as a Viet Nam veteran by the Department of Labor.

8. Enter name of state which the registrant calls home.

9. Enter long title of apprenticeable trade. Example: Camera Repairer. Entries are limited to those apprenticeships authorized by the Commandant of the Marine Corps.

10. Enter 9-digit DOT code which matches the apprenticeable trade entered in Item 9. The Work Processes Schedule indicates this code.

11. No entry required.

12. Self-explanatory.

13. Self-explanatory.

14. Enter name and address of command forwarding application.

15. Enter total term of the apprenticeship (required hours for completion). Example: 6000. The Work Processes Schedule indicates the total term of the apprenticeship.

16. Enter hours of creditable work experience completed prior to registration, if any. A registrant may be credited with 1000 hours of previous work experience for each full year that his/her service record validates assignment to an MOS applicable to the apprenticeable trade. Applicable MOSs, if any, are listed at the bottom of the Work Processes Schedule for each authorized apprenticeable trade. However, credit for previous work experience completed prior to registration cannot exceed more than 50% of the term of the apprenticeship. Therefore, no more than 3000 hours of previous work experience can be credited to a 6000-hour apprenticeship. Portions or fractions of years of work experience will not be credited.

17. Enter the difference between Item 15 and Item 16. This difference is the number of work experience hours which must be completed by the apprentice.

18. Enter any comments regarding previous work experience, future assignment or next duty, or further explanation of any above item. Entry not mandatory.

19. Signature of commanding officer, education officer, or his authorized representative.

20. Title of registrar who signed Item 19.

21. Enter date that Item 19 was signed. This will be the effective beginning date of the apprenticeship.

Enclosure (1)   16

APPRENTICE WORK EXPERIENCE HOURLY RECORD (1500)
NAVMC 11015 (3-77)
SN: 0000-00-006-6840 U/I: SH

APPRENTICE NAME *(Last, first, middle)*

1. Print legibly.
2. Enter completed hours daily or weekly.
3. Have Supervisor verify hours at the end of each week.
4. Keep this record in your Work Experience Log.

WEEK OF	DATE FROM						DATE TO					SIGNATURE & TITLE OF SUPERVISOR																
DAY	LETTERS IDENTIFIED IN WORK PROCESSES SCHEDULE																										**TOTAL HOURS**
	A	B	C	D	E	F	G	H	I	J	K	L	M	N	O	P	Q	R	S	T	U	V	W	X	Y	Z	
SUN																											
MON																											
TUES																											
WED																											
THURS																											
FRI																											
SAT																											
TOTAL HOURS																											

WEEK OF	DATE FROM						DATE TO					SIGNATURE & TITLE OF SUPERVISOR																
DAY	LETTERS IDENTIFIED IN WORK PROCESSES SCHEDULE																										**TOTAL HOURS**
	A	B	C	D	E	F	G	H	I	J	K	L	M	N	O	P	Q	R	S	T	U	V	W	X	Y	Z	
SUN																											
MON																											
TUES																											
WED																											
THURS																											
FRI																											
SAT																											
TOTAL HOURS																											

WEEK OF	DATE FROM						DATE TO					SIGNATURE & TITLE OF SUPERVISOR																
DAY	LETTERS IDENTIFIED IN WORK PROCESSES SCHEDULE																										**TOTAL HOURS**
	A	B	C	D	E	F	G	H	I	J	K	L	M	N	O	P	Q	R	S	T	U	V	W	X	Y	Z	
SUN																											
MON																											
TUES																											
WED																											
THURS																											
FRI																											
SAT																											
TOTAL HOURS																											

Enclosure (2)

WEEK DATE FROM	DATE TO	SIGNATURE & TITLE OF SUPERVISOR
OF		

DAY	A	B	C	D	E	F	G	H	I	J	K	L	M	N	O	P	Q	R	S	T	U	V	W	X	Y	Z	TOTAL HOURS
SUN																											
MON																											
TUES																											
WED																											
THURS																											
FRI																											
SAT																											
TOTAL HOURS																											

LETTERS IDENTIFIED IN WORK PROCESSES SCHEDULE

WEEK DATE FROM	DATE TO	SIGNATURE & TITLE OF SUPERVISOR
OF		

DAY	A	B	C	D	E	F	G	H	I	J	K	L	M	N	O	P	Q	R	S	T	U	V	W	X	Y	Z	TOTAL HOURS
SUN																											
MON																											
TUES																											
WED																											
THURS																											
FRI																											
SAT																											
TOTAL HOURS																											

LETTERS IDENTIFIED IN WORK PROCESSES SCHEDULE

SIGNATURE & TITLE	DATE

PERSONAL HISTORY

LAST NAME	FIRST NAME	MIDDLE INT.
RANK SOCIAL SECURITY NUMBER		DATE OF BIRTH DAY/MONTH/YEAR
PLACE OF BIRTH		
PERMANENT HOME OF RECORD		

SIGNATURE OF APPRENTICE   DATE

_____   _____

MILITARY EDUCATION

COURSE TITLE	LOCATION	LENGTH FR:	TO:
Basic Electrical Course			
Journeyman Electrical Course			
Other Related Courses:			

Total Education Hrs:	1st Year Hrs:	Certified	2nd Year Hrs:	Certified	3rd Year Hrs:	Certified

CIVILIAN EDUCATION

HIGH SCHOOL OR GED/	NAME, ADDRESS, ZIP CODE/ GRAD. DATE

COLLEGE OR GED/	NAME, ADDRESS, ZIP CODE/ GRAD. DATE

VOCATIONAL SCHOOLS

LIST ALL SEPARATE COURSES TAKEN

LIST ALL OTHER SPECIALIZED TRAINING NOT COVERED ABOVE

MILITARY ASSIGNMENT

UNIT	ADDRESS	FROM	TO	DUTY ASSIGNMENT

CIVILIAN OCCUPATION

LIST ALL CIVILIAN RELATED EMPLOYMENT COVERING THE LAST TEN (10) YEARS RELATING TO: Electrican		
FIRM; NAME AND ADDRESS	NO. YEARS	POSITION HELD

WORK EXPERIENCE FOR _____
(YEAR)

	Jan	Feb	Mar	Apr	May	Jun	Jul	Aug	Sep	Oct	Nov	Dec	Total For Yr	Int
A														
B														
C														
D														
E														
F														
G														
H														
I														
J														
K														
L														
M														
N														
O														
P														
Q														
INT														

A. Hand Power Tools
B. Special Purpose Equipment
C. Blue-Prints
D. Distribution Panel
E. Connect Switches
F. Junction Boxes
G. Conduit Systems
H. Interior Wiring
I. Load Balance
J. Fixtures

K. Conductor Polarity
L. Grounding
M. Transformers
N. Fuses
O. Single Phase Motors
P. Poly Phase Motor
Q. Motor Controllers
R. Operational Tests
S. Maintenance

CERTIFICATION OFFICIAL _____

TITLE _____

Enclosure (8)

APPRENTICE PROGRESS/STATUS REPORT (1500)
NAVMC 11014 (3-77)
SN: 0000-00-000-6840 U/I: SH

1. Print or type.
2. Prepare in triplicate.
3. Forward original and one copy to CMC (Code OTTE) with attached photo of last Hourly Record of Work Experience.
4. Apprentice retains one copy in Work Experience Log.

PRIVACY ACT NOTIFICATION

To be filled in by Apprentice or official in accordance with instructions on reverse side.

1. NAME OF APPRENTICE *(Last, first, middle)*   2. SSN   3. SEX ☐ MALE ☐ FEMALE

4. RACE/ETHNIC GROUP
☐ CAUCASIAN/ WHITE   ☐ NEGRO/ BLACK   ☐ AMERICAN INDIAN   ☐ SPANISH AMERICAN   ☐ ORIENTAL   ☐ INFORMATION NOT AVAILABLE   ☐ NOT ELSEWHERE CLASSIFIED

5. Did you serve on active duty on or after 5 August 1964 and before 8 May 1975?   ☐ YES   ☐ NO

6. HOME OF RECORD *(State)*

7. Apprenticeable Trade in Which Registered   8. Total Hours for Term   9. Hrs. Preregistration Experience   10. Hrs. Completed Since Registration   11. Hours Remaining

TO: Commandant of the Marine Corps (Code OTTE), Headquarters U.S. Marine Corps, Washington, D.C. 20380

12. FROM *(Activity submitting report)*

ACTION REQUESTED

(check one)

13. Please suspend registration for the apprentice named above for the reason(s) checked below:

   a. ☐ Orders to light duty
   b. ☐ Nature of current assignment prohibits work in apprenticeable trade for one year or less
   c. ☐ Hospitalization
   d. ☐ Operational commitments prevent reporting for progress interview

14. ☐ Please lift the suspension of registration for the apprentice named above effective: _____ *(Date)*

15. ☐ Please cancel the registration of the apprentice named above for the reason(s) checked below:

   a. ☐ Commanding officer's prerogative
   b. ☐ Discharge or release to inactive duty
   c. ☐ Termination of work experience for one year or more
   d. ☐ Death
   e. ☐ Failure to report for twice-a-year apprentice progress interview
   f. ☐ Personal request of apprentice

16. ☐ The apprentice named above has completed all required hours of work experience in all areas of the apprentice trade. A "Certificate of Apprenticeship Completion" requested.

17. SIGNATURE OF APPRENTICE   18. DATE

19. SIGNATURE AND TITLE OF OFFICIAL   20. DATE

31

INSTRUCTIONS FOR APPRENTICE PROGRESS/STATUS REPORT

Item No.

1. Self-explanatory.
2. Enter Social Security Number. Example: 399-03-6433.
3. Self-explanatory.
4. Self-explanatory. Must agree with Item 5 of apprentice registration.
5. Entry must agree with Item 7 of apprentice registration.
6. Enter name of state which the apprentice calls home.
7. Enter long title of apprenticeable trade. Example: Camera Repairer.

ITEMS 8, 9, 10, and 11 NOT REQUIRED IF SUSPENSION (Item 13) OR CANCELLATION (Item 15) IS REQUESTED.

8. Enter total term of apprenticeship as indicated on Work Processes Schedule. Must agree with Item 15 of "Apprentice Registration Application."

9. Enter number of verified hours of work experience completed prior to registration. Must agree with Item 16 of "Apprentice Registration Application."

10. Enter cumulative number of hours of work experience completed as a registered apprentice. Attach reproduced copy (photostat or xerox) of every "Work Experience Hourly Record" which shows hours completed since last report.

11. Add Item 9 and Item 10 and subtract total from Item 8. Enter result in Item 11.

12. Name and address of activity from which report is submitted.

13. Check if this is a request for suspension. Suspension retains the apprentice in a temporary inactive status for no more than one year. Request for suspension requires signature of apprentice in Item 17. A request for a suspension may be mailed directly to Commandant of the Marine Corps by apprentice. No suspension will be carried longer than one year.

14. Check here if reason for suspension no longer applies. A request for lifting suspension requires signature of apprentice in Item 17 and signature of Commanding Officer or Education Officer in Item 19.

15. Check here is this is a request for cancellation. Cancellation removes the apprentice from the apprenticeship program. A request for cancellation requires signature of Commanding Officer or Education Officer in Item 19.

16. Check if apprentice has completed all required work experience, both grand total of hours and total hours in each skill area. A check in this block must be supported by final entries in Items 8, 9, 10 and 11, plus a produced copy of the "Work Experience Hourly Record" completed since the last apprentice progress interview or report. Hours of verified work experience completed before registration (Item 9), if any, will be distributed equally among the skill area of the trade. A check in this block requires signatures in Item 17 and Item 19.

17. Signature of apprentice required for Items 8, 9, 10, 11, 13, 14, 15f and 16.

18. Date in which signature of apprentice is affixed in Item 17.

19. Signature of commanding officer or education officer submitting report required for Items 8, 9, 10, 11, 13, 14, 15a and 15f.

20. Date on which signature in Item 19 is affixed.

Certificate of Completion of Apprenticeship

United States Department of Labor

Bureau of Apprenticeship and Training

This is to certify that

has completed an apprenticeship in the trade of

SAMPLE

in accordance with the standards recommended by the Federal Committee on Apprenticeship

DATE COMPLETED

William H. Kolberg
ASSISTANT SECRETARY FOR MANPOWER

SECRETARY OF LABOR

Hugh C. Murphy
BUREAU ADMINISTRATOR